DREAMS of BRANDON

A Mother's Journey through Grief and Loss

GALE HENDERSON

ISBN 979-8-88943-444-3 (paperback)
ISBN 979-8-88943-445-0 (digital)

Copyright © 2024 by Gale Henderson

All rights reserved. No part of this publication may be reproduced, distributed, or transmitted in any form or by any means, including photocopying, recording, or other electronic or mechanical methods without the prior written permission of the publisher. For permission requests, solicit the publisher via the address below.

Christian Faith Publishing
832 Park Avenue
Meadville, PA 16335
www.christianfaithpublishing.com

All Scripture passages used in this manuscript are taken from the New King James Version.

Printed in the United States of America

*Blessed be the God and
Father of our Lord Jesus Christ, The Father of all comfort,
Who comforts us in all our tribulation
That we may be able to comfort those who are in any
trouble with which we ourselves are comforted*
—2 Corinthians 1:3–4 NKJV

To my children, Brandon and Erika—my heart's joy
In memory of Eric, my children's dad

*To children who suffer from mental illness. God sees you.
The struggle continues.*

To my husband, Wayne—for his love and devotion

To my sister, Sheri, who suggested I keep a journal
to help me in my grieving moments

April 1, 1985

Brandon's Story

"Brandon's middle name is Jeremiah," my ex-husband boasted when Brandon was born. He had one finger pointed to heaven, like a Baptist preacher.

We named our son after the Old Testament prophet Jeremiah. Jeremiah was called the *weeping prophet* because he grieved over Israel's rejection of God's prophecy given through him. Jeremiah was ignored, overlooked, and dismissed by all who knew him. He had none of what we in our culture would label success—fame, riches, popularity, or influence. But God chose him to be his prophetic voice at a time of great upheaval, impending sorrow and subjugation for his chosen people, the Israelites. He chose Jeremiah because of his obedience and his persistence in informing the people of the impending doom through Babylonian captivity.

Brandon Jeremiah was unknown—an adolescent boy struggling with a debilitating mental illness until the end of his life. As I transcribe my dreams for God's glory, I know why I chose Jeremiah for my son's middle name. I could not foresee my child's destiny when I gave birth to him joyfully on that spring day thirty-seven years ago, but the Lord knew. He knew Brandon's time on earth would be brief and mental illness would plague him until he called his name. But my son's life had purpose despite its brevity, as do all children.

Brandon Jeremiah's purpose was for his death to be used by God to comfort grieving parents when their own children would die. I am a testament to it. God has given me a vision, and my writing today demonstrates the Lord's healing power and the reassurance of life eternal through Jesus Christ, the Almighty God. My child's death was the catalyst for this book. It encompasses my moments of grief, my tears, and my joys as I move through life without one of my beloved children. It was Jesus—the only true God—who helped me through it.

Brandon Jeremiah's onset of mental illness began when he was thirteen. We noticed changes in his behavior and ability, particularly in his motor and cognitive skills. Brandon Jeremiah was diagnosed with schizophrenia. Like the Prophet Jeremiah, he was not famous, but he knew God. At church, he would clap his hands to the music, even though it was getting exceedingly difficult to sit still and to listen. Jeremiah the prophet cried because of his love for Israel. I wept for my Jeremiah because of my love for him and the grief I endured over his passing. God did not remove the prophet Jeremiah from his isolation, nor did he remove schizophrenia from my Jeremiah. But both found favor with God, and in their circumstance, God used them for his mighty purpose and his grand design.

The prophet Jeremiah found favor in God's eyes, a favor that is not measured by human standards but in the light of God's love and infinite mercy, which cannot be extinguished. The prophet Jeremiah was called from this life and did not live to see the enslavement of his people, the Israelite nation. He was a prophet who received a vision from God. This vision foretold of dark days for the people of Israel.

Centuries later, in another place and time, a young man by the same name would be born and die. He, too, will not witness the contribution his small light made in the world. In their lives, as well as our own, God is the potter and we are the clay. If we are pliable and open to his Word, he can create a grand design that cannot be shattered or extinguished. God is still sovereign in all things. He will bring his perfect will to pass, even if we are nonparticipants. Triumphantly, God's Word tells us nothing can separate us from him, neither life nor death—what was, what is, and what is to come can never separate us from the love of God through Christ Jesus. I believe this and take immense joy and comfort in it. Do you? If so, then take comfort in this reality. Your child now knows true love and freedom in heavenly places.

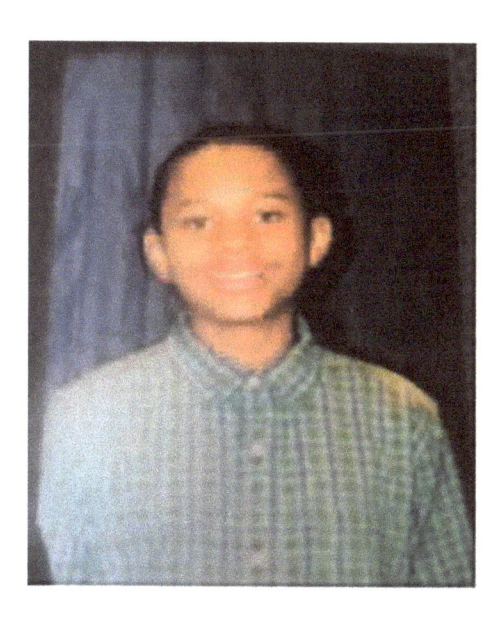

Preface

This book is written to console parents whose children have died at a young age. It addresses the impact of death from God's perspective through the holy Bible. My son, Brandon Jeremiah, left this life in 2002, and the implications of his death remain two decades later. With his death, I'm reassured that God knows our pain when he calls our little ones home. He will ease the burden of grief (not remove it) with words of love, comfort, and promises of eternal life.

I was a brokenhearted mother, who had lost her only son, and my grief was unbearable. But in my brokenness, I turned to my faith in God, my Savior and redeemer, for relief.

My writing represents God's consolation and the reassurance of his love for me and my child, who is now before him.

Dreams of Brandon: A Mother's Journey through Grief and Loss details visions of my child through dreams. I have recorded them for nearly twenty years. My dreams, which strengthened me and mended my broken heart, were from God. This book also sheds light on Brandon's struggle with mental illness, which altered his life until the end.

The death of our children is a traumatic and debilitating experience. It is a story I'm compelled to share. Out of great pain, I rise. In doing so, I hope to lift another parent from grief's stranglehold, to share the truth of God's Word and the reality of his love in the most life-altering and tragic event of our lives—the death of a child.

Acknowledgment

Gale's Song of Praise to God
September 22, 2017

Glory, majesty, honor, power, and strength to my God, who was, who is, and who is to come—
World without end.
From glory to glory, time immemorial, you are God.
Creator, loving Father, Savior, provider, healer, protector, the alpha and the omega! The righteous one—
You are Lord Jesus.
Blessed be your name forevermore. Let all the earth sing your praises.
Let all the angels and the heavenly host continually worship and adore you.
For you are worthy, my God and Savior, of my praise and devotion; I acknowledge your sovereignty.
I acknowledge my need for you.
I need your grace and mercy. I love you, Lord Jesus.
Jesus, Jesus, Jesus—
Oh, how I love the name of Jesus!
It soothes my restless soul. It is a healing balm for my weariness
For all my days, I am thankful to my God for his faithfulness—
His loving-kindness toward me.
If I had a thousand tongues, I could never express the joy I have when I think of you—
What you did for me on Calvary.
Because of you, I know truth, and that truth is Jesus.

I am free.
The world no longer binds me.
Jesus paid a high price for my freedom.
Yes, my Savior and God, you are worthy of my praise and adoration.
    Use my life for your glory.
Let me be your hands in the earth. Hallelujah!
I will continually sing praises to my God.
I will haste unto his throne as long as I live, in this life and the next.
Amen.

Introduction

On the death of our children—the pain is profound and as deep as the ocean. My child is dead. There are no words to express the magnitude of my grief. Death is irrevocable. My child's bright smile has vanished. His laughter is forever gone. His voice lives only in memory. The hope for his future has dissipated. There will be no graduating from high school, college, getting married, and having a family of his own. The old photographs reflect his image and have become mere proofs of his short existence on earth. There is a vacant chair situated around the dinner table. It beckons an occasional glance from the family, who are keenly aware of the void. Deafening silence has replaced the lively conversation of teenagers. What remains is the silence of a child who is grieving the loss of a sibling.

One room in my home is now ominously quiet. The drawing tools and typewriter have remained untouched. The bedroom door is closed—indicating the occupant will never return. The form of a sleeping teenager is now gone. The silence bears witness to his passing. Now there is no one inquiring, "Mama, what's for dinner?" or asking for a new Nintendo game.

The doctor's visits have ceased. School is over indefinitely. There will be no more awards for his talent in sculpting or giving his mother a big hug. The opportunity for second chances is but dust. The breath that animated him has ceased. My child's time on earth is finished. Death.

Brandon was my only son. He died at seventeen years of age.

Chapter 1

Love Never Dies

Time does not erase the gravity of a child's death. It lingers and stays with us for our lifetime. I am writing this book for grieving parents. Parents of minor children who are no longer with us. The answer is simple. *Love never dies.* It does not matter how long ago the tragedy happened. Time is of no consequence. In a parent's mind, a child's death is as fresh today as it was yesterday or decades ago. No truer statement exists for parents who are now in grief's grip. God's Word was my strength when my child died. Scripture references are meant to lift you up and support you. Read, refer, and meditate on them. God's Word will strengthen and console you as you grieve.

Jesus our Savior is the source of all comfort (2 Corinthians 1:3–4). When our children precede us in death, it affects us emotionally, physically, and psychologically. We are paralyzed with grief—it takes our breath away. It feels like our tomorrows are gone and we are in a suspended animation, unable to function. Grief has us in a stranglehold. Life has come to a standstill. Our children are gone before their potential is realized. It is a reality we can never predict, entertain, let alone rationalize. Our children are called from this life at times without warning or preparation. They are gone, and the pain is more than we can bear.

Time brings acceptance and healing of the heart, but the void will always remain. Prepare for this reality. Memories will replace the physical child, and these will have to be enough. We don't have a choice in this matter. The power of life and death is beyond our scope as humans. We cannot control when, where, and how we die, or our age when we leave. No manner of medical science can give us immortality. It belongs to God alone, and he is with us even until death (Matthew 1:18–21).

Men and women process grief differently. Women are conveyors of humanity. It is through our bodies that humanity continues. Humanity is born of a woman (Genesis 4:1). However, men are God's vessels to plant the seed. Scripture is clear (Genesis 4:1). A special bond is formed between mother and child, and this bond should never be underestimated. I contend the death of a child will be felt and processed differently by women. Brandon's father and I responded very differently to the loss of our son. I write from a mother's perspective of grief, not from a clinical analysis of death. *You* refers to all parents.

Death lifts up our eyes to God for answers, when it has claimed the greatest gift he has given us—our children. In this book, experience rules the day. I live with my son's death one day at a time through God's grace. The Lord brought me through those difficult years. He imbued me with clarity of thought and peace of mind when both evaded me (John 14:27).

God's love came shining through when I needed it the most. Grief could have overwhelmed me if not for Jesus my Savior. His reassuring presence through the Holy Spirit and the Bible (which is the living Word of God) comforted me in my grief (Matthew 5:4).

God's people surrounded me and my family when the trajectory of our lives was forever altered. The Word of God is referenced throughout this book. Its purpose is to bring you comfort and reassurance in a world that has been turned upside down. Death has called your baby to himself, and God has received him or her.

Chapter 2

The Journey Begins

Now that your child has died, what do you do? I will tell you what you do not do: self-destruct. Life will go on for you until God calls our names in death. But in the meantime, you must continue living. You have many responsibilities—yes, even as you grieve. You may be a stay-at-home mom or dad, who is juggling a career or other pursuits and has children who lost their sibling. They will need your care and attention now more than ever. Who's going to be strong for them? I had my daughter to raise when her older brother and only sibling passed away. She was now an only child, which I know impacted her deeply. My spouse and I divorced the following year, so I had to raise our daughter alone. She was fourteen years old at that time.

My marriage did not survive after our son's death, but it does not mean yours will not. When I look back on those difficult years, I know there is a God. My faith in his Son, Jesus Christ, sustained me because I allowed him to. Grief cannot be perpetual. Joy will come in God's own time, if you allow it. True love and joy come only from God and his son, Jesus (Jeremiah 31:3). Even in the midst of my circumstance, I had to face down my fears to push forward without my son and husband. God spoke to me, through his Word, that his love is enough to carry me through the turbulent sea I now face (1 John 4:18). The Word of God healed my broken heart (Psalm 34:18). Otherwise, grief would have consumed me.

As I grieved, I prayed to God and asked him, "Why my son? Where is my child?" I had so many unanswered questions for God. I was confused and disoriented after Brandon died. I remember praying to God for my child's healing, and death came to him instead.

God's answer wasn't what I expected, so I had many questions for God at that time. God answered everyone in ways only he can. His Word eased my fears and reassured me of life after death (John 14:1–3). "Why my son?" As I previously mentioned, Brandon suffered from mental Illness. Even though I prayed for healing, his condition didn't change. I desperately wanted Brandon to have a normal life of a teenager. But God's answer wasn't what I expected.

In his mercy and love, the Lord ended my child's suffering in death; he answered my prayer in the light of eternity. Why did he not heal him and permit his life to continue? I do not know. I do know God does not make miscalculations. His vision is all-encompassing. He is omnipotent. Jesus, not Satan, holds the keys to life and death. Everything, including death, is subject to his authority (Matthew 28:18).

Brandon's suffering was as difficult for him to bear as it was for us to witness. His illness created great sadness in our hearts and prevented him from living a normal life. His education required a specialized curriculum and schools to accommodate his disability. Brandon was a gifted artist—a talent we were not aware of until his art teacher presented us with a sculpted head of Carter G. Woodson, Father of Black History, that Brandon made. He was a twelve-year-old sixth-grader, and the illness had not yet manifested. Brandon had been working on the sculpture for a while and had been wanting to surprise us. He won first prize for his creation. We were stunned, to say the least. He had the gift of sculpting.

His award-winning piece of art is a centerpiece in my home. But in hindsight, Brandon knew something was terribly wrong. He asked me many times the question: "Mom, what is wrong with me?" I tried to explain the diagnosis.

Why did my child have to endure this debilitating mental disorder and die so young?

God answered my question with scripture and reinforced my love for him. "Good people pass away; the Godly often die before their time. No one seems to care or wonder why. No one seems to understand that God is protecting them from the evil to come" (Isaiah 57:1 NLT). My beloved son was now in perfect peace. Amid his illness, we could do nothing but love and support him unequivocally.

Brandon's life required many adjustments. Friends didn't come easy because they didn't understand mental illness. He was medicated to help with his disability, but truthfully, they weren't effective. His dad and I were at our wits' end as to what should be done. I turned to God out of sheer futility. My son's suffering was beyond our control. However, I now know God's Word is sufficient, even when our prayers for healing on behalf of our children aren't answered the way we expect (Hebrews 4:16). Whatever the outcome was, I committed his life to God. I knew he was in God's hands now. But we could not foresee the eventual outcome.

Chapter 3

Indestructible and Enduring Love

Sickness and evil are not of God but of Satan. God permits them to bring about his perfect will and to draw us closer to him, but he is not the initiator. Job was a righteous man in the sight of God. He had God's favor and was blessed with wealth, land, and family (Job 1:1–4). Nonetheless, he was subjected to Satan's attacks. God permitted it to show Satan that Job would never curse him through death and destruction (Job 1:1–18). Job was steadfast in his faith in God, even through his circumstance (Job 1:18–20).

The Holy Spirit led me to the book of Job to reassure me Brandon's transition in the eyes of God was an answered prayer. The Lord has freed Brandon from Satan's attack, whose entire purpose is to kill and destroy God's creation—humanity (Hebrews 2:14–15). God loves his son, Jesus, just as much as I love my son, Brandon. God didn't save Jesus from death either (Mark 15:24–27). But he raised him up to be Savior, king of kings, and Lord of lords over all creation, and a living sacrifice for our sins by submitting to death on the cross (Hebrews 2:9). Writing this book reveals God's purpose for my son's life. "All things work together for good for those that love God and are called according to his purpose" (Romans 8:28).

Children are beloved by Jesus (Mark 10:15–16). They are a gift from God (Psalm 127:3). The Bible states that we belong to God, no matter our physical state (Romans 14:8–10). It is sin that creates a great division between humanity and God. But God sent the remedy in the person of Jesus Christ to reconcile that division 2,000 years ago (John 3:10). No power on earth can separate us from the love of God (Romans 8:34–39). We have God's promise that our children are with him, in his glorious presence, when they die (Psalm 23:4).

Chapter 4

Visitation

In the years following Brandon's death, God has allowed me glimpses of my son through dreams. It was another method God used to heal my broken heart. God is infinite (Psalm 102:12). Jesus is God (Titus 2:13–14). He is limitless. He is not bound by time or space, so he can do what he wants, when he wants, and for whom he wants (Romans 9:14–16). I wrote down my dreams and recorded the images as soon as possible while they were still fresh in my thoughts.

My son comes at various stages in life. At times, he is small, and at other times, he is older. He is always beautiful, vibrant, and inquisitive. At times, there was communication, and at other times, there was none, only images. I expressed my love for him and told him he is missed. In some dreams, he speaks with the same loving response: "I love you, too, Mom," and at times, there is no communication at all. Some dreams are brief with only his fleeting image. I awake, and he is gone. In some dreams, he is working, doing what he loved to do while on earth, that is, making or doing something with his hands. He always appears without evidence of illness. Since I cannot put twenty years of my dreams of Brandon in this limited space, I will only reveal a few.

Dreams are powerful tools used by God to communicate to us. God communicated to Joseph through dreams to inform him of the inheritance he was to receive because of the promise he made to his grandfather Abraham. God always keeps his promises to his people from generation to generation (Genesis 28:12–14). God showed Joseph through dreams that his brothers will kneel at his feet and be subservient to him. They despised Joseph and resented his dreams. Jealousy and anger motivated his brothers to sell him into slavery and then to tell his father, Jacob, he was killed. The brothers reinforced the lie by returning Joseph's beautiful robe stained with animal's blood to their father—a further proof of the deception (Genesis 37:31–32).

Joseph was sold into slavery in Egypt, but despite his circumstance, the favor of God was on him. Joseph was purchased by Potiphar, an officer of Pharaoh.

Joseph was a good worker and was successful in whatever he did because the Lord was with him (Genesis 40). Potiphar took note of this and made Joseph his personal attendant, which elevated him to supervisor of the entire household. However, Joseph caught the eye of Potiphar's unfaithful wife, who wanted more from him than just keeping the books and running the household. When he refused her advances, she falsely accused him of sexual impropriety. Joseph was thrown into prison (Genesis 39:19–22).

By God's providence, two years later, the Pharaoh of Egypt had a dream he could not interpret. The king's adviser knew of a man who could interpret the dream—that man was Joseph.

While in confinement, Joseph interpreted the dreams of two inmates. Each interpretation was correct—one of the men was executed, and the other was pardoned (Genesis 40). The king ordered Joseph's release and summoned him. Joseph interpreted the dream as a warning from God that the kingdom will undergo severe famine and great prosperity, each for a seven-year interval. Just as God warned Pharoah through dreams of the impending starvation of his people, he gave Joseph the gift to interpret them.

Fast-forward to another Joseph. God spoke to Joseph, the Virgin Mary's betrothed, to ensure him of Mary's fidelity, even though he knew the child, Christ, was not his. He informed Joseph in a dream that the child she was carrying was conceived by the Holy Spirit, not by man (Matthew 1:18–21). She was carrying the Savior of the world, and he need not be ashamed of her or harm her in any way.

God intervened to give Joseph peace and reassurance concerning Mary, who was in an untenable situation. He did this through a dream.

My dreams of Brandon ushered in healing from the death of my child. Each time I open my eyes to the dawn, I simultaneously feel both joy and sadness—the latter because Brandon's death exposed my grief and the former because my dreams allowed me to see my child and be with him again. I am grateful to God for every glance and conversation. Just to see my boy once more brought me immeasurable peace. I know the Lord permitted me a glimpse of my child and his place in eternity. This is how I know my dreams were from God.

Chapter 5

Renewal and Reassurance

My prayer for parents is to find the strength not just in yourselves but in God to help you heal during this time of tragedy and grief. Jesus is the great healer of our hearts and our bodies (Psalm 27:8). Jesus, God, and the Holy Spirit are one and the same (John 10:30). Jesus left us the Holy Spirit when he went to be with God the Father so we will never be alone on this road called life (John 14:16–18). It is a very real presence for those who believe and trust in the only living Son of God, Jesus Christ (Matthew 3:16–18). Your child is with him. Brandon is with him. This is my peace and my hope. It can be yours too. Just ask God to help you and believe his Word.

My hope is that you come away from reading this book with peace, love, and reassurance that all is well with your child. Even though you can no longer see him or her in this physical world, they have transcended. The essence of who they were is not buried in the ground nor burned through cremation. That essence has gone to its creator (Romans 14:7–9).

The only living true God and his Son, Christ our Lord, who is in all, through all, and above all (John 1:14).

Healing takes time, and God is aware of this. He weeps with us when we are in pain (John 11:33–35). Be patient with yourselves. There will be sleepless nights in the early days after your child's passing. Death has visited you and created an enormous and seemingly insurmountable vacuum in your life. A vital link has been severed. It will take a long time to come to a place where you can reflect on the child that is no longer by your side, and on this day, you will smile. But only God can bring this to you through his loving Son, Jesus. Just because you can't see a thing does not mean it doesn't exist. This is a cruel deception Satan perpetuates in our world. You will not get proof. It takes great faith and acceptance of what cannot be changed, altered, or seen. According to the Scripture, faith is the substance of things hoped for and the evidence of things not seen (Hebrews 11:1).

Just because your child no longer exists on this earthly plane does not mean he or she isn't. There is a heaven—beautiful and lovely beyond our comprehension. There are no words to describe how awesome it is. In the Book of Revelation, John explains what he saw (Revelation 1). This is the place where our children now reside.

Through the Lord's healing power, I learned that I can let go of Brandon. He is experiencing pure joy, and I desire no less for my child. I no longer wish he was with me because this existence brings pain and suffering. When he was alive, my son suffered greatly. Without reservation, I know he has found pure joy in God's glorious presence. One day, I will join him, and I will experience this new existence in God's presence. My faith in the Lord has sustained me. He is faithful to those who trust him at a time when kind words and condolences only dull the pain and cannot bring healing of mind and heart (Lamentations 3:23).

DREAMS OF BRANDON

Dreams of Brandon: A Mother's Journey through Grief and Loss is my story. It is a revelation of the brevity of life and the confluence of death, children, and dreams. This is my journey after my son died unexpectedly. His death rocked the very foundation of our lives. We were never the same after his passing.

This book represents God's healing power through dreams. Praise God! God used the greatest tragedy of my life to draw me closer to him. He will do the same thing for you—if you allow him to.

Guilt and remorse enveloped me, but God's love for me interceded. To God be the glory for his indelible mercy and loving-kindness toward me. He allowed this child to be born to me, and now he has called him home. What a gift and a privilege it had been to give birth to him and to raise him. Hope, joy, and laughter have been restored. With God's promises, I now have confidence that everything is alright (Psalm 94:18–19). My Brandon is just where he should be. God has spoken. All is well.

Now, my dreams of Brandon—

GALE HENDERSON

October 29, 2002

Dear Brandon, my son,

    I don't understand why your life was so short. I'm in great anguish over this. I question myself and look to God for answers. I asked him why you died so young, why you are gone. I struggle with these thoughts. I don't believe I will ever know why your life was so brief.

All my love,
Mama

DREAMS OF BRANDON

November 11, 2002

My son,

Dealing with your death is exceedingly difficult. I recently returned to work and took a break at around 3:00 a.m. I began to think of you, your life, your journey, and when it ended. I wept softly, lost in my private thoughts. The nursing staff was unaware of the grief that stifled me.

Suddenly, a feeling of reassurance swept over me—a tiny voice spoke within me. It wasn't audible, but I heard it.

> *All is well with your son. Cry and mourn him as a mother should, whose child is no longer physically present with her. God knows and understands your pain. Weeping is necessary, but be at peace. Rest assured Brandon is well. His pain is no more. You can be sure of this. He is happy and in perfect paradise. Your separation from him is only a temporary state, not eternal. You will see your child again.*

Immediately, my tears ceased, and a calm came upon me—but only for a time. I'm sure those words of solace and encouragement came from above. Even so, I know my grief will never stop as long as I live.

Love,
Mama

GALE HENDERSON

January 4, 2003

Dear Brandon,

    Happy New Year, my child! It's clear that you are near, even though I can't see you. I think of you every day. I miss you dearly. I'm writing this early in the morning because you came to me in a dream.

    In the dream, I was in the living room of my childhood home. I was alone. There was no furniture. There was only a TV. I was grieving your loss. Even though I couldn't see you, I sensed your presence and concern for me.

    Then your sister came to console me. She said, "Mom, Brandon wasn't very happy, but now he is."

    Your image then materialized and was projected on the wall, like an old movie reel from decades past.

    Next, our family stood in front of a large crowd. People were cheering on your dad, and he was so proud of you. He clapped for you, looked at you, and pushed you out front. He introduced you to the crowd. You were so bashful, and you looked back at your family. You loved it and stepped back in line with the rest of us.

    Next, the scene changed. You and your sister were listening to the speaker behind the podium. You were dressed so handsomely—my young man in a suit and tie.

    Then I awakened.

    Son, thank you for visiting me in my dreams. This is the first dream I've recorded. I believe this is God's way of healing my broken heart and your way of letting me know all is well. Every day, you are in my thoughts. Your memory lives in and through me. This will never change as long as I live. It will take many years for this agony over your passing to subside. You are my baby—my precious son.

    When people ask me how many children I have, I say, "Two, but one has passed on." But the truthfulness of my response is precarious. Your spirit is always here. In my dreams, I see you all the time. I will continue to write down my dreams when you come again.

Mama

DREAMS OF BRANDON

February 16, 2003

Dear son,

    Thank you for visiting me in my dreams last night. It was so good to see you. We hugged and expressed our love for one another. It was a beautiful dream. I can't imagine the peace and joy you are now experiencing in God's presence. But I know you are happy and your pain is no more. None of us know when we will depart this life. In my grief, I say that you left us too soon. But God knew the time and place, and he is never wrong.
    Son, you will be in my heart and mind for as long as I live. I love and miss you, my baby.

Love,
Mama

July 30, 2003

My son,

I saw you so vividly last night. My heart was overjoyed to see my child again. It was so real. It seemed like you were here with me. I was not in a deep sleep when my bedroom door was opened slowly. You walked in. You looked ethereal, not solid in form. But you were just as I remembered, only radiant. You crossed the room and sat on the edge of the bed. I sat up to greet you. There was such a joy in my heart. I hugged you, and surprisingly, my hands didn't pass through you. I expressed how much I love you and how I've missed you every day since you left.

You replied, "I love you, too, Mom."

I wanted to hold that moment in time. I saw your face up close—a mother and a son holding one another's gaze. In that instant, I awoke, and you were gone.

I smiled. My baby was here. Thank you for coming, son. I thank God for allowing you to come and see me. It has been a while since your last visit, and this has brought me such joy. I know one day we will be reunited. God promised. But I miss you dearly in the meantime.

We are doing fine. No matter where we are, you will always be a part of us. You will always be my loving son. That bond will never be severed. Yes, it's true that the physical bond has been broken, but the spiritual bond can never be severed by death. I know in the fullness of time, I will be reunited with my baby again.

The Lord is perfect. He doesn't err. It was your time to make life's final journey. Enjoy paradise, Brandon. I can't imagine its beauty, basking in the Lord's love and radiance for all eternity. It must be so. What place but heaven can hold the spirit of my beloved Brandon, a wonderful son and a beautiful young man while on earth.

I love you always,
Mama

DREAMS OF BRANDON

May 13, 2004

My dearest son, Brandon,

It was so good to see you again this morning in my dreams. I was somewhere between consciousness and sleep. I was lying in bed, and your face appeared—so close and clear. I reached to hug you, and you hovered over me, just staring. Then you spoke and asked me if I will always take care of you. I said I will. You made me promise. When I reached out to kiss your cheek, your face was transparent. It was as though I was kissing the air. As I awakened, I felt something on my face, like a feather that catapulted me out of my sleep. You faded away. But I could still here you say, "Do you promise?"

As I opened my eyes, I responded, "I promise."

Son, your visits bring me such joy and such sadness, when I awake and realize you are gone. If only I could stay within my dream for a little while longer.

Until we meet in eternity,
Your loving mother

GALE HENDERSON

September 16, 2004

My dearest son, Brandon,

I dreamed. It was so good to see you again. It has been a long time since you visited me in my dreams. I've wondered when I would see you again, and here you were. This time, I was sitting at the bedside with a dying nurse. We worked on the same hospital unit, and her name was Rita. Recently, the staff was informed of her passing. But in my dream, she was on her deathbed. I sat with her and comforted her for what we both knew was the inevitable outcome. We talked. I spoke of you—your death and my grief.

Suddenly, you appeared in the doorway. You did not speak a word to alert me you had arrived, but instinctively, I knew it was you. I asked you to come forward so I could introduce you to her, and you did. I hugged you, and I said to Rita, "This is my son, Brandon, who died two years ago."

She shook your hand, and you stepped back. I went on to tell her what a fine young man you were and how God helped me through the grief of losing you. I opened my eyes.

Brandon, my son, my baby, thank you for coming to help ease her fears about death. I miss you dearly, baby boy.

Erika got her senior pictures, which was taken on Saturday. Dad is okay. I'm doing well, son.

You're always in our hearts, Brandon. Even though your physical life was short-lived, the memories you left behind are forever—until we meet at the end of our journeys.

My love always,
Mama

DREAMS OF BRANDON

October 12, 2009

My loving son,

    You were in my dreams again. I was lingering, but I didn't know why. I stood outside a store, waiting for something or someone. I was becoming anxious, waiting for what seemed like an eternity. At that moment, you appeared in the doorway, but you turned back, like you forgot something. You were a little boy. In a moment, you returned. I lit up when I saw you, and somehow, I was keenly aware that my vision of you was fleeting. I was correct because in an instant, I opened my eyes.

    You are gone—only memories remain. I smiled—relishing your visit. My child, you are never far from my conscious and unconscious mind. Your presence is sorely missed, especially by the woman who bore you. Keep visiting me, even if words are never spoken. The Lord is so gracious and full of tender mercies. Even getting a glimpse of you pacifies my grief and brings me fleeting joy. I love and miss you dearly as the years go by.

I love you always, Brandon,
Mama

GALE HENDERSON

May 2, 2011

My dearest son,

This dream was so vivid. I was looking for you. I managed to find you sitting by a lake. You were carrying a book bag. When I called you, you stood up and started running toward me. You were a teenager. We were so happy to see one another. We embraced and began our walk together. I awakened.

It was so good to see you once more. Thank you, son, for coming to easy my grief and sorrow. Once again, you brought joy to my heart, which has a gaping hole since you left us. I love you always.

Mama

DREAMS OF BRANDON

February 20, 2012

My dearest son, Brandon,

    I saw you in my dreams once again. My car was in the garage. But when I opened the back door, it wasn't there. I assumed it was stolen, but I didn't know how since it was in the garage all night. I panicked and went outside to see if I could get a sight of the thief and my vehicle. Nothing. When I turned around to head back inside, I heard an engine behind me. Slowly I turned around only to see my car parked on the street; its engine was running, and its windows were up. The tinted windows obscured my view, so I couldn't see inside. As I approached the vehicle, the passenger side window slowly rolled down.

    Imagine my surprise when I saw your smiling face in the driver's seat. Oh, what joy I felt to see my son's face again! Thank you for bringing my car back, although you may have just borrowed it and took it for a spin, like most teenagers do. I love you, son, and I miss you. Everyone is well. There's just one missing piece—you. I will see you on the other side.

Your loving mother

GALE HENDERSON

March 28, 2012

My dearest son,

    I saw you in my dreams last night. Oh son, it's always good to see you. You were younger in the dream, no more than twelve years old. I watched you, hugged you, and gave you a big kiss on the cheek. How I miss you as the years go by. My mother's heart still grieves. I know it always will. Keep coming, son. You are never far from me. Your memory remains, and your face is as vivid as the day you left us. I love you always.

Mama

DREAMS OF BRANDON

September 29, 2012

My dearest son,

In this dream, I was asleep. You opened the door with a blanket in hand, which you laid over me. You then turned and left quietly. I opened my eyes.

It was so good to see you and to experience your love. You are still watching over your mother, even beyond the great chasm that separates us. You are in my thoughts every day since you died. I just thank our God, who is wise, beyond all knowledge for blessing me with you for a time. My love always, son.

Mama

GALE HENDERSON

June 10, 2013

My loving son,

    You were in my dreams again last night. It was so good to see you and to speak with you. I never wanted to wake up—my slumber is a doorway for a reunion with my beloved son. It was wonderful. I had so many questions, and you answered them all. I remembered asking about heaven, but for the life of me, I can't remember your answer. I asked about the color of the trees. Again, I couldn't remember your response. Just to see and spend time with you was more than enough. Oh, the joy I felt! I was so overjoyed to see my child again that your answers were lost upon me. We were together a long time, mother and son. You talked a lot, and I listened. You were so happy and handsome. I still miss you terribly and even more as the years go by. My heart will never recover from your early exit from our lives. There is, without a question, a missing link in this chain of life, one that I will never reconcile.

Love,
Mama

DREAMS OF BRANDON

November 20, 2014

My dearest son, Brandon,

    Here you are once more. As always, my heart was filled with joy and gladness to see you. Son, it's been well over a decade since you've been gone, and much has happened in our lives. I dreamed you were standing on the balcony of this beautiful home. I pulled up in the driveway, looked up, and saw you. You called out to me from the balcony. I ran upstairs to greet you, but when I reached the balcony, you disappeared. I wept. I miss you terribly, but I'm dealing with your passing. I love you, baby boy. I will see you again when my time comes. Love you, son.

Mama

March 2, 2015

My dearest son, Brandon,

    These journal pages are fading with time. Many years have passed since you died; however, my sorrow endures. But I'm encouraged and rest assured of God's promise that death is not the end. I looked at your picture today, reminiscing. I remember our love for you and your love for us, your family. Love remains. It hasn't dissipated with time. However, an ever-present void lingers because my child is gone. You are in paradise with our Lord Jesus, and he loves you more than I ever could. You have completed your course. I love you always.

Mama

July 2, 2015

My dearest son, Brandon,

The years are going by so fast now, and you are missed more today than the day you said goodbye. My child, my sweet boy, the unbelievable has evolved into a stark reality. Still, the full gravity of it is difficult to express. My sorrow never ceases on this day of all days. It is like a perennial flower, which returns to full bloom each year—a constant reminder of what I no longer have. God knows my grieving mother's heart, and even though I have come to terms with your loss, I shall never forget. You are never far from me. You remain a star burning brightly in my heart and in my memories. Enjoy God's magnificent presence. Earth has no sorrow that heaven cannot heal. Neither pain nor strife exists.

Your peace is perpetual. In God's presence, joy is complete and is beyond human comprehension. Glory to his name. I know it to be true, Brandon.

I've lived my life based upon this simple truth, and it has sustained me. God be glorified for his unfailing love through Jesus Christ our Savior and redeemer. You are sorely missed.

Your loving mother

GALE HENDERSON

July 4, 2015

My dearest son,

    This dream was vivid. Seeing your beautiful smile filled my mother's heart with joy. We were at my childhood home, which no longer exists. I did not notice you at the door, but Wayne nudged me and directed his gaze toward the front door. I hesitated to get up from my seat. But when I got to the door, you were behind the screen waiting to be invited in. Oh, my baby boy, the joy I felt to see my oldest again was beyond description! I snatched you inside and hugged you so close. I asked you where've you been and that I was so happy to see you again. You returned my embrace and said the same. I awoke abruptly.
    You were gone once again, living only in memory. God is still sovereign, no matter how I feel. The anniversary of your death rekindles my sorrow. I miss you terribly. I will hold on to my dreams of you. I will be seeing you.

Mom

DREAMS OF BRANDON

July 12, 2015

My Brandon,

    The dream was fleeting. After several years of writing my dreams of you, an unfathomable void remains. You were in a shadow—not clearly visible, but I knew it was you. A mother knows. In this dream, I was overcome with grief, and I wept. Oh, my son, I see your face often in my dreams. You are never forgotten. You will always be with me—as it should be. Love you, baby boy.

Mother

GALE HENDERSON

January 31, 2017

My dearest son,

Thank you for your visitation last night. We embraced one another—mother and son. I was overjoyed to hug my child once more. You looked younger, and we were on our way to visit your sister. When we arrived, you called to her from the car, and she appeared on her patio. You could see the happiness on her face when she saw you. She came down to greet us. There was a group of dancers, and we all joined in the celebration. We had such a wonderful time. I awoke.

The years have passed by quickly, son. It has been fifteen years since you've passed on, and you have been missed every day since. The world has changed. I believe you were spared the hardship and lack of empathy this life surely would have imposed upon you. God is merciful.

Mama

DREAMS OF BRANDON

April 1, 2017

My dearest son,

    Today would have been your thirty-second birthday. Happy birthday, my handsome young man. The years have passed, but you have not faded from my memory. You are as vibrant and lasting in my thoughts as the last day I saw you seventeen years ago. You are gone. I have accepted your death in my heart. I no longer cry when I look at a photograph, but the separation is very real. I remember how much you were loved and how you loved your family. But I now know you dwell in God's presence and death is a transition—that life exists after this one ends. I reflect on what might have been and commit your spirit to God's loving arms.

    I dreamed of your grandparents last night. Very strange. Somehow I know you are together. I haven't seen you for some time. But it's alright. I believe as the years pass by, my dreams of you will become less frequent, and so they have. God orchestrated the dreams when my heart was broken and in need of mending. Due to God's grace and love, I no longer worry about how I will go on without you. God knows, and so do you. I believe earthly concerns are not part of eternity. You are forever free, and I will see you again someday. I love you, son. I haven't forgotten. I lit a candle for you today as always on your birthday.

Love,
Mama

June 3, 2018

My dearest son,

This is the last entry I will write in my grief journal. After seventeen years, the Lord has given me a vision. He has revealed the purpose for you being born and dying so young. The mission is to comfort parents whose young children have died. I want parents to know God's love for them and the children who have transitioned. Over the years, I have poured out my heart into these pages, expressing my grief and recording dreams of you, while acknowledging God's grace amid it all. Now, I'm ready to lend my story to help parents with their grief. This is what the Lord has brought to fruition in my life. He has taken the focus off me and has turned it toward him. To God be the glory! Forever he reigns!

My pastor, the late bishop Dennis Leonard of Heritage Christian Center in Aurora, Colorado, once said during one of his sermons: "Use the greatest tragedy in your life for God's glory and watch what he will do." Brandon, your death was my life's greatest tragedy.

The bishop's sermon brought to remembrance my child's death and writings in an instant. The Lord said to me in my spirit as I sought his direction in prayer, "The seed has already been planted. Now reap the harvest for the glory of God and for his kingdom."

God had revealed his purpose for your death. I have my answer and am compelled to implement God's plan for me. I love you, son. It is not yet my time. But as sure as I breathe today, it will come. We will then celebrate together in God's glorious light, love, and grace with Jesus at the center of it all. My beautiful baby boy, my loving son, my gift, my dreams of you are practically nonexistent now, but look at what I have gained in your place—God's favor, peace, and grace. I have your sister, who has grown into a wonderful woman, and a supportive husband—they are far more valuable than monetary reward.

DREAMS OF BRANDON

Thank you, Lord, for my son's love and for his presence on the earth for a little while. Thank you for my dreams of him that sustained and healed my broken heart. Praises be to the Father, the Son, and the Holy Spirit—the blessed Trinity who was, who is, and who is to come. My heart is healed by God's power and mercy. My joy and laughter have returned. There is no more need to record my dreams or pour out my grief on fading pages. God's purpose for my son's life and mine is fulfilled. It has been revealed. As I continue in this life, know, my son, that you are always with me. Your face is indelibly etched in my memories—the love I have for you can never be displaced nor extinguished. Praise God! He is good. His love endures forever in every situation. God gave you to me as a gift, but you were never truly mine. You belonged to God. All praises to the Lord Jesus Christ for his healing power, restoration, and care for a grieving mother. Thank you, son, for your love.

Until we meet in eternity,
Mama

Conclusion

God will use dreams to reveal and reassure us of his presence. He did it for Joseph, Jacob, Abraham, and people of faith throughout the centuries, myself included. God is infinite and not bound by time or space. He is our eternal designer and knows us quite well. We came into being by his word; his breath is in our lungs.

My dreams of my deceased child gave me peace when grief consumed me.

However, everyone approaches the death of a child differently. Not everyone will experience this connection with God because people do not know him or seek him. My perspective is one of faith in God and his gift of eternal life through his Son, Jesus Christ, upon whom our salvation depends. I trust him with my life, and all that I have belongs to him—including my children.

Brandon is gone from this earthly plane, but I know where he is. Brandon had a bright smile and an amicable spirit. He was and always will be our beloved son and brother. However, God loved him more and called him home on a warm summer day.

Brandon's flame flickered and extinguished quickly. God knew the time and place to call him home. His will is perfect and sufficient, even in the most dire and tragic circumstances of life. The Book of Ecclesiastes tells us there is a time and purpose for all things under the heavens—a time to be born and a time to die, a time to plant and a time to reap, a time for joy and a time for sadness, a time to laugh and a time to weep. The Word of God is immutable. It changes lives and demonstrates the true meaning of love.

Your child is with God now. He's with Jesus—in his magnificent light. God is the Father of light. His love is unfathomable and knows no boundaries.

We all seek and want to be loved. God is love, and that love is clearly demonstrated through the sacrifice of God's Son, Jesus, who laid down his life as a ransom for many. According to God's Word, there is no greater love than for one to lay down his life for another. Those who seek truth and yearn for the disclosure of light amid darkness are drawn to God. According to the Word of God, the only way to enter God's presence is through his beloved Son, Jesus. Jesus said in the sermon on the mount, "Blessed are they that mourn, for they will be comforted."

God's comfort in the midst of tragedy is free. We need only humble ourselves and call on him.

God has wiped every tear from our children's eyes, and they know nothing but pure joy and love in heavenly places. With death, their bodies have returned to the earth and their spirits have soared heaven bound into the arms of our Lord. Our children are clothed in heavenly garments, not bound by time nor space. They are now perfect before our creator. God is their focus now, not the turbulence and sorrows of this earth. This should give you great peace. I know it does for me.

God loves you and knows your pain. Submit to him and accept his outstretched arms of comfort and reassurance. The time spent with your child will remain with you forever. It is not lost to death. Death is a doorway, a transition point. With it begins a new reality not seen by our naked eye until it closes permanently to this world. Love is eternal, and God, through Jesus Christ our Lord, is the true source. Jesus is the true vine, and the branches that connect to him will not wither. Furthermore, the fruit (God's people) that grows from these branches is consistently renewed in the driest desert and torrential storms. God is with you, and he holds your child until you see him or her again. It will be alright.

Read the following poems given to me by a mourner at my son's funeral. I've read both innumerable times through the years. Now I share these reassuring words with you.

> Death is Nothing at all. I have only slipped away into the next room. I am I, and you are you. Whatever were to each other, that we still are. Call me by my old familiar name, speak to me in the easy way you always used.
>
> Put no difference in you tone, wear no forced air of solemnity or sorrow. Laugh as we always laughed at the little jokes we enjoyed together. Pray, smile, think of me. Let my name be ever the household word that it always was, let it be spoken without effect, Without the trace of Shadow on it. Life means all that it ever meant. It is the same as it ever was; there is unbroken continuity.
>
> Why should I be out of mind because I am out of sight? I am waiting for you, For an interval, somewhere very near,
>
> Just around the corner. *All* is well.
>
> (Henry Scott Holland, Canon of St. Paul's Cathedral 1918)

> To those I love and To Those Who Loved me
>   Now that I am gone, release me, let me go
> I have so many things to see and do You mustn't
>   tie yourself to me with tears,
> Be thankful for our beautiful years
> I gave you my love, you can only guess How
>   much you gave me in happiness

I thank you for the love you each have shown,
> But now its time I travel on alone

So grieve a while for me, if grieve you must, Then
> let your grief be comforted by trust

It's only a time that we must be apart So bless the
> memories within your heart I won't be far
> away, for life goes on

So when you need me call and I will come Though
> you can't see me or touch me I'll be near, And
> if you listen with all your heart you'll hear

All my love around you soft and clear
And then, when you must come this way alone,
I'll meet you with a smile and say "Welcome Home"

(Author unknown)

May the peace of God that surpasses all understanding keep you in all things. May memories of your child remain with you always, filling you with great joy and love. Finally, may you trust in God's promise of eternal life for those who believe in Jesus Christ our Redeemer. Your child's journey is complete. He or she waits for you. God bless you immensely.

The end

DREAMS OF BRANDON

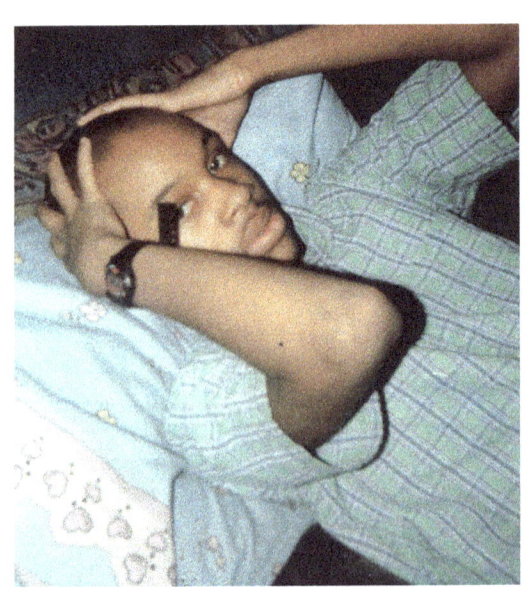

GALE HENDERSON

DREAMS OF BRANDON

GALE HENDERSON

DREAMS OF BRANDON

About the Author

Gale Henderson is a follower of Jesus Christ. She enjoys being outdoors and taking long walks, especially in spring, when nature has rejuvenated. She loves the aesthetics of God's creation—the beauty of mountains, waterfalls, rainbows, and quiet streams. The changing colors of trees in the fall make this season a close second favorite. She loves flowers; her favorites are lilies and peonies. She is an ardent gardener and grows a variety of flowers and vegetables, particularly each spring. She considers her garden a sanctuary, a testament to God's provision.

She loves history and holds a bachelor of arts degree in this field from the University of Dubuque, where she graduated top 10 percent of her class. She is a founding member of the newly established Hope City Church of Colorado in Aurora, CO lead by founders Pastors Marlon and Tamera Saunders.

She resides in Denver, CO.

Printed in the USA
CPSIA information can be obtained
at www.ICGtesting.com
CBHW052006140824
13132CB00058B/1036